Beyond the Law of Attraction to Real Magick

How You Can Remove Blocks
to Prosperity, Happiness and
Inner Peace

(Text and Workbook)

Moonwater SilverClaw

A QuickBreakthrough Publishing Edition

More copies are available from the publisher with the imprint QuickBreakthrough Publishing. For more information about this book contact: askawitchnow@gmail.com

This book was developed and written with care. Names and details were modified to respect privacy.

Disclaimer: The author and publisher acknowledge that each person's situation is unique, and that readers have full responsibility to seek consultations with health, financial, spiritual and legal professionals. The author and publisher make no representations or warranties of any kind, and the author and publisher shall not be liable for any special, consequential or exemplary damages resulting, in whole or in part, from the reader's use of, or reliance upon, this material.:

Other Books from Quick Breakthrough Publishing:

- Be Heard and Be Trusted: How to Get What You Want
- Nothing Can Stop You This Year!
- Darkest Secrets of Persuasion and Seduction Masters
- Darkest Secrets of Charisma
- Darkest Secrets of Negotiation Masters
- Darkest Secrets of the Film and Television Industry Every Actor Should Know
- Darkest Secrets of Making a Pitch to the Film and Television Industry
- Darkest Secrets of Film Directing
- Darkest Secrets of Small Business Marketing

Praise for Moonwater SilverClaw:

"When I first met Moonwater I realized what a remarkable, compassionate person she is. Over time, I've seen how she works hard to kindly serve and encourage others through her spirituality and found myself moved by her dedication. She brings Wicca to life, enveloping you in the mystery and magick of the Craft. Her writing talent is amazing! Her kindness and even sense of fun is ever present throughout her writing. Moonwater expresses profound Wicca concepts through examples in her own life experience. Wicca actually saved her life. and empowered her to leave an abusive marriage, and this shows the power of this sacred path to positively change the course of our lives, too. Moonwater's stories personally inspire me, and I am confident that they will inspire you also."
– Rev. Patrick McCollum, internationally recognized spiritual leader working for human rights, social justice, and equality; the 2010 recipient of the Mahatma Gandhi Award for the Advancement of Pluralism.

"Moonwater's writing will give you a portrait of a woman who lives her faith, and whose life was saved by it. Because so many lives, my own included, were irrevocably changed by Wicca, were given new focus, new purpose, and perhaps most importantly, new personal power to realize one's dreams and ambitions. . . . It's a story about making your own happy endings, about rescuing yourself, and that, I believe, is what makes writing like this necessary."
– Jason Pitzl-Waters, blogger at WildHunt.org

"Moonwater's writing is like sharing a nice cup of coffee with a new friend, while you two are taking a walk in the woods. As a writer, Moonwater has found her Voice. And that voice has a LOT to teach all of us, from the young person who wants to know why she feels 'special ', to us seasoned practitioners of Wicca who can always benefit from a straight-forward review of the basics." – Angus McMahan, blogger, http://www.patheos.com/blogs/askangus/

Visit Moonwater SilverClaw's blog:
www.TheHiddenChildrenoftheGoddess.com

CONTENTS

DEDICATION AND ACKNOWLEDGEMENTS

This book is dedicated to the God and Goddess. Thanks to Sherry Lusk, Kay Pannell, Stacy D. Horn, and Tom Marcoux for editing. Thanks to Judita Bacinskaite for rendering this book's front cover. Thanks to the readers from over 92 countries of my blog: TheHiddenChildrenoftheGoddess.com

BEYOND THE LAW OF ATTRACTION TO REAL MAGICK

Imagine you could get what you really want! When I first heard about the Law of Attraction, it sounded great to me. In fact, it was in line with training I had in my spiritual path. But then I heard of so many people feeling gravely disappointed when their attempts to use this Law failed.

In essence, the Law of Attraction states: "Like attracts like." So if you can get your thoughts to a positive and resolved state, you can attract positive outcomes into your life.

But then a number of people found that after doing a bunch of meditating and affirmations, they still did *not* get what they desired. What was going wrong?

In this book, I will help you remove blockages that must be dealt with *before* the Law of Attraction can work for you.

This book includes the missing parts to make the Law of Attraction actually work.

How do we increase the odds of your desires coming to fruition dramatically? This book will help you take the next step to **real magick** to get real results in life!

I believe that how people often try to use the Law of Attraction is broken. That is, they do *not* have the complete story. No wonder they're disappointed that their desires go unfulfilled.

On the other hand, this book actually faces the idea that the Law of Attraction *is* magick. People need the rest of the story in order align with this Law and get what they need.

We'll cover the blockages to true success. We'll focus on financial abundance, *and* you can use the techniques here to apply to *various aspects* of life.

So what really blocks us from the prosperity we want? Our self.

Some of us are confronted with self-esteem issues. We'll deal with that and more.

Let's take the next step.

SELF-PERSPECTIVE: OVERCOME THE BLOCKAGE OF NOT FEELING WORTHY

Do you feel worthy of the best that life has to offer? Maybe on the conscious level you say, "Sure. Bring it on. The new house, new car, and a real, loving relationship."

But have you ever sabotaged your chances of getting exactly what you wanted?

Self-sabotage can occur because of feeling not worthy on a subconscious level.

If it's subconscious, how can we deal with this?
Good question.

Soon I will share with you a Self-Love meditation.

But first let's talk about magick. The whole premise of this book is that there is a way to go about the Law of Attraction with more power.

To put it simply, the Law of Attraction is a form of

magick, but people who read an introductory book on the Law of Attraction are often denied enough information to truly make the Law of Attraction work in their own lives.

So to really make a positive difference in your life, we need to talk about real magick. I spell magick with a "k" to distinguish it from stage magic you see on television.

Magick is a natural power, *not* a supernatural one. Who uses magick? In my spiritual path, Wicca, one is trained to use magick in appropriate ways.

When Wiccans do magick, they channel *natural* energies and create change with them.

Well, if Wicca isn't really supernatural, then why practice Wicca at all?

To put it simply, *you want something*. That's probably why you were interested in the Law of Attraction in the first place. Now in the context of learning real magick, you'll be able to fully use the Law of Attraction. And that's good news!

Everyone is different and has their own answer to that question. I like to think of religion as a bottle of wine. Let's say you have three different people who all taste the same bottle of wine. The first person points out that the flavor has accents of oak. The second praises the hints of apple in it, and the third enjoys the floral notes. They are all right. The wine contains all the flavors they described. But each person detected something different. Religion is like that. Deity can't be entirely known. So the truth of it is scattered into many faiths.

In Wicca, we honor the God and the Goddess. If that's new to you, you can substitute the label of Higher Power or God or Deity.

The Gods and Goddesses have helped me and they can help you, too. The first thing they taught me was self-love.

Before we go further, let's make a distinction between self-love and self-conceit (or being stuck in one's ego).

Self-love is about kindness and support. So it's a good thing. It is NOT about your ego or puffing yourself up.

Let me show you how the Gods changed my perspective on myself for the better.

One of the best exercises I learned is meditation. Through reflective meditation, the Gods helped me understand how skewed my perception of myself really was. This was a key turning point for me.

One thing you always hear about are affirmations, but for many of us these just don't work.

First, let's cover what an affirmation is. It's a personal, positive statement. It can be as simple as "I feel terrific" or "I make a lot of money."

For many, the above statements don't work. Why?
A number of people have told, "It just sounds like I'm lying to myself."

Like myself, many people's inner self-beliefs interfere with these positive statements. For an example, if I used the affirmation "I am thin," my brain would object with "No, I'm not. Look in the mirror." It's not true. No matter how hard you try to pound that new idea into your brain, your brain pounds just as hard back.

So how did the Gods help me deal with this problem? They inspired me to create a Self-Love Meditation.

So instead of the uphill battle of an affirmation, we'll use the Self-Love Meditation to work with the situation.

[You can work with this meditation by audio recording it in your own voice and then play it back. Or you invite a friend to read this section to you.]

Self-Love Meditation

Close your eyes.

Breathe in and out deeply . . . Relax.

Keep breathing.

Breathe out the stress of the day.

Breathe in relaxation and peace.

(Pause)

You are still aware of the light that is in the room.

Now the light begins to fade.

As it fades you feel total comfort. You feel safe and secure in the darkness.

(Short Pause)

Now, a new form of light blossoms. It surrounds and wraps you in its loving energy. This light is the light of the Gods.

It is a light of love and compassion. Take it in.

As you take this light and understanding in, you can now see with the Gods' eyes.

You can now see yourself as they see you, pure, beautiful, whole. You are a masterpiece of their creation. You were made with love, and you are a manifestation of their love. You are love.

This understanding fills you.

(Pause)

With this new understanding you are now ready to return to the physical world.

You know that even though you may leave the light at this time it is never truly gone.

It's a gentle transition as the light begins to fade around you.

Slowly at first. It gets darker and darker.

As it fades you feel total comfort. You feel safe and secure in the darkness.

(Short Pause)

Then a familiar light returns, the light in the room where you started.
It gradually gets brighter and brighter.

You are back in the room. You have brought the calm and peace and happy feelings back with you.

Now, gently open your eyes.

You can do this meditation as often as you need to. It may not take at first, but keep trying. Eventually the Gods' light will shine within you.

What results did you get the first time you tried the meditation? What did you experience?

_____

_____

_____

_____

_____

_____

_____

Moonwater SilverClaw

SELF-ESTEEM

How would you describe your self-esteem? Okay? Good? Bad? For much of my life, I'd say that my self-esteem was truly low.

My childhood was filled with physical and mental torture perpetrated by my older brother—and my parents' neglect. Somehow I survived to my sixteenth year.

One day, I walked into a Barnes and Noble bookstore in my hometown. Earlier that year, I had heard a new word, Wicca, so I asked the sales clerk, "Do you have any books on Wicca?" Her eyes lit up, and with great excitement she led me to a shelf and started pouring books into my arms.

That evening, alone in my room, I started to read Scott Cunningham's book, *Wicca: A Guide for the Solitary Practitioner*. My heart filled up. I had finally found my home.

Now I reveled in a new world. Soon I was meditating, and after some sessions, the Gods made contact with me.

The Gods embraced me with pure love. My body filled up with their love for me. It moved from my head through my entire body, down to my fingers and toes. Happiness was so foreign to me; I had never felt this way before. But I shifted to a deep part of myself I hadn't known, where I knew that I was one with the Gods. Forever.

The Gods found me beautiful. They took pride in me.

I never knew anyone could have this much love for anyone, especially me! This epiphany was a brilliant light into my chasm of darkness and despair. Now I could start to see myself for what I really was worth.

With this knowledge, I found a new confidence in life. Once the Gods opened me up and shone their loving light in me, I was transformed into love—love for myself and for others.

The "harm none" concept of Wicca rang true for me. I didn't want anyone to go through what I had endured. I wanted to treat everyone with respect, compassion, and love. So I started on my path and became a Wiccan priestess.

It's a beautiful path.

I want to emphasize that the "An it harm none" concept (The Wiccan Rede) not only applied to not hurting others, but it also included not hurting myself.

Before I connected with the Gods and Goddesses, I believed that I wasn't worth the dirt I stood on. At that time

I was so sure of it!

Then, I met the Gods. What they showed me didn't match what certain people had been showing me my whole life. My brother called me "Piggy," although I weighed only 112 pounds at the time. I later learned that he was full of garbage. The Gods showed me that I was made perfect, even if the world around me called me broken. I chose to believe in the love of the Gods.

I discovered that magazines that tell me I'm too fat and not beautiful enough are liars! I don't have to be a size 0 to be beautiful and happy. I don't have to use their creams and gels to improve my looks. I just have to be me. With the Gods' help, I can better see the world. I can see situations more clearly and more positively.

What thoughts are stopping you from success? As you see from the above my thought process was damaged. I was listening to the wrong people in my life and not seeing the true me. I felt I didn't deserve success because I wasn't worthy of anything good.

If you're hurting right now and you feel that your self-esteem needs a boost, I have a couple of suggestions:

1) Make space to do something spiritual (perhaps, a ritual) everyday. The point is that for many of us, the way to feel the Gods' and Goddesses' compassion is to pause and actually do something that connects you with them. It can be as simple as lighting a candle or sitting in silence for even just 5 minutes (meditating).

2) Pause and consider how you can act in a new compassionate way toward yourself. How would you act to comfort a dear friend who was hurting? Would you provide a good meal? Invite him or her to watch a video to escape for a couple of hours? Would you take a walk in nature with your friend?

How can you bring a new compassion for yourself into your life? What compassionate actions do you wish to try to bring some soothing and support into your life?

_____

_____

_____

_____

_____

_____

_____

_____

GROUNDING

Now that we explored some reasons why we are blocking our own way, let's explore how to lead ourselves toward success and financial abundance.

Grounding I have found is a great way of getting rid of those negative energies that come with the lack of self-esteem. You learn to shunt the negative energy into the earth safely. With this process you will be able to *lighten your burdens* from the negative energies that come from negative self-thought. Here is how to do grounding:

Imagine you're feeling upset and you'd really like to let go of built-up negative energy. Your answer is to ground yourself. Grounding is the process of giving up or getting rid of your negative and unwanted extra energy. This process sends this energy back to Mother Earth so that she may cleanse it and recycle it back into the universe.

For example, one year I had a particularly unpleasant conversation with my sweetheart. He was all stressed out about working hard at his job and doing our taxes paperwork. He wanted acknowledgment for all he was doing. But I was taking it as if he was blaming me for not doing enough.

After a few cross words, we retreated to different rooms. I wanted to ground myself, so I did a Tree of Life Meditation (described in the next chapter). It worked. I returned to my sweetheart and hugged him. And we both went on to enjoy the rest of the evening.

Knowing how to ground successfully enhances our well-being. Grounding keeps us happy and healthy both physically and mentally. It cleans out our negative and unwanted energy. When used in conjunction with meditation, it is known as "Grounding and Centering."

Grounding Exercise

The simplest form of grounding is to place your hands on the bare Earth. Breathe in deeply. As you exhale, push your extra energy out of your body and into the Earth. As you do this, envision all the negative or excess energy in your body being taken back safely into Mother Earth for her to recycle and use as she needs. You should feel balanced and refreshed after doing your grounding exercises.

If this grounding exercise doesn't work for you, try hugging a tree. Trees are great at taking your unneeded energy and shunting it down safely into the Earth.

Practice grounding every day. You can ground yourself before going to work or school. Many Wiccans find it helpful to ground themselves before stepping inside their home, particularly if they have had a stressful day.

Before you enter your house, place your hands on the Earth to rid yourself of the negative energy you acquired that day. As an alternative, you may also take off your shoes and stand on the soil.

Remember to check how you are feeling throughout the day. If you need to ground, then do so. You'll find that grounding keeps you feeling refreshed and calm all day!

As we come to the conclusion of this chapter, I want to provide you with two scenarios in which grounding is very useful:

a) Sometimes, we have too much energy, even if it is positive energy. I recall the time I forgot to ground after a particularly rigorous ritual that left me with way too much energy. I was bouncing off the walls for days. You may think this is funny, but you try going to work with zero sleep!

b) Some forms of negative energy tax you with "weight" like a sack of cement. When you ground yourself, you release such energy, and you suddenly feel lighter and free. You will live a happier life.

Finally, the true benefit of grounding is to, in essence, refresh your energy. It's like having a river clear out a stagnant pool of water. Grounding truly is a cornerstone of Wiccan practice.

Question: When and how can you implement this grounding technique into your life? How about scheduling time in your day planner or PDA?

_____

_____

_____

_____

_____

_____

_____

_____

CONFIDENCE

Meditation

Now that you know about grounding we will continue with more details about meditation. Realize that meditation is calming the mind and using it in some cases to connect to Deity.

Below I will share the Tree of Life Meditation. Please know that people who meditate regularly just radiate a calm, *confident* energy.

The Tree of Life Meditation

Slowly breathe in and out. Breathe in the energy of love and peace (envision this as white energy). Breathe out all stress and negativity (envision this as black smoke). Keep taking deep breaths in and out. Concentrate on the white energy being breathed in and filling up your body with loving energy. Then let go and breathe out the negative energy you see as black smoke. As you do this, release the stresses of the day. Repeat this breathing cycle at least three times until you are comfortable and relaxed.

As your body and mind begin to relax, continue deep breathing and focus on this image:

Envision roots made up of energy sprout from the bottoms of your feet. With each breath, extend the roots farther and farther down toward Mother Earth.

Extend them down through the floor, down past the plumbing of the house, and down, down deep into Mother Earth's body. Go down to her core, to the center of her heart.

Once there, with each breath in, pull up the energy from Mother Earth. Breathe out the stress, and breathe in the blue-green energy of the Mother.

Pull the energy up through your roots, up past the plumbing of the house, past the floor, and into your feet. The energy feels clean and refreshing.

Breathe in deeply. Pull the blue-green energy up into your legs and past your knees. Pull it up, up into your Root Chakra at the base of your spine. Let it fill your body, going up, up into your Sacral Chakra and continuing to your Solar Plexus Chakra. Breathing in deeply, draw the energy up, up into your Heart Chakra. Let the energy flow down your arms and into your hands. Feel your body relax as the energy fills it.

Breathing in, draw the energy up into your Throat Chakra.

Concentrate on the blue-green energy filling your body. When you are ready, with another breath in, breathe the energy up into your Third Eye Chakra.

Using your breath, draw the energy up into your Crown

Chakra. Feel the energy flow throughout your body.

With another breath in, pull the energy up and out of your head. The energy forms like branches toward the Sky above you. Continue and let the branches flow up to the universe and out into the cosmos.

Draw down the golden energy of the Sky and universe into you. Continue to let the Sky energy intermingle and mix with the Earth energy that is already there. Pull it down through your body and into your arms.

Continue breathing deeply, mixing and pulling the energies down to your Heart Chakra.

Breathe in again, pulling the energy of the universe down into your Solar Plexus Chakra.

Continue pulling in the energy. Let it flow into you. Pull it into your Root Chakra. Breathing deeply, pull it down your legs and down to your feet.

Feel the energy from both the Earth Mother and the Sky Father that is within you. Enjoy this relaxing and cleansing energy.

In a moment or two, slowly start to pull your branches back within you, pulling them in with each breath.

Let any extra energy dissipate through the roots that you had placed into the Earth from your feet.

Now breathe the roots up, and back into your body just like the branches that were above you. Give yourself over to the total relaxation you now feel.

In a moment or two—and when you are ready—open

your eyes.

* * *

Use the above *Tree of Life Meditation* to introduce calm and balance into your life.

As we come to the conclusion of this chapter, here are a few more thoughts about chakras, which function as our energy centers. When properly maintained, they produce healthy energy. It is this healthy energy that produces the physical body's aura. An aura is the energy your body radiates.

Having a weak aura or having bad spots in your aura usually means that one or more of your chakras are out of whack. A sick or weak aura screams that the person's chakras are not working properly; it is an indication that his or her chakras need work.

Meditation is important for replacing the stagnant energy in your body's chakras with clean-flowing energy. It is good not only for our aura but also for maintaining a healthy state of mind. Meditation flushes out unwanted, excessive, or negative energy with healing positive energy.

Consider a daily practice of The Tree of Life Meditation. You will find peace within yourself, and the world will look a little less hectic. This meditation lowers blood pressure and reduces stress. You can practice technique as often as you need it.

How can you implement The Tree of Life Meditation in your life? What times of day would work best for you?

Will you get up 10 minutes early? Will you do this in the garage just before you enter your home (if you have kids)? What benefits do you see with this technique?

_____

_____

_____

_____

_____

_____

_____

_____

_____

HOW TO FREE YOURSELF FROM PEOPLE (AND PAST RELATIONSHIPS) THAT BLOCK YOUR SUCCESS AND PROSPERITY

How to Heal by Separating Yourself Spiritually from a Bad Relationship

We've all been in a bad relationship at some time in our lives. Whether it is a family problem or ex-lovers or a friendship that just plain went sour. So how do we spiritually separate ourselves from these poisonous people?

You can use many different ways to accomplish this. However, the first and foremost thing to do is to verbally end the relationship. You might say something like: "I don't think this is healthy for us. So let's just stop seeing each other."

Second, physically stay away from the person. The idea is to stop spiritually ingesting the poison of interacting with them.

Many people hesitate to do the first two steps. For many, true change is quite difficult. I can relate to this. And, I'm providing the below ritual for when you're truly ready to move on with your life.

Now, it's time to use what I call the Separation Ritual. This ritual involves disconnecting the astral connections that you and the person made during the relationship. I personally know that this is valuable. In fact, my spiritual training empowered me to release myself from an abusive marriage.

Unless you take action, you stay connected to the person. How? Your astral bodies remain connected. Negative energy can still be transferred both ways. To protect yourself from these bad energies you must cut all ties from that person. This is where the Separation Ritual comes in.

Ideally, the person would participate in a Separation Ritual with you. That often does not happen. So you take an object that will stand in for the person. This object could be a picture or even a teddy bear, if the person likes teddy bears.

Use a length of yarn or piece of red string, which represents the connections you have between you and the toxic person. Red is for the life force but you can uses another color if you think that would be a better representation.

For this ritual you'll need both your athame (a knife to cast your circle) and a boline, which is a white handle knife used specifically for cutting physical objects during ritual.

Important: Athames are used to cut energy. Bolines are used to cut physical objects.

Here are the steps of True Separation:

1. Verbally end the relationship
2. Stay away from the person.
3. Ground yourself.
4. Cast circle (described in detail later in this book).
5. Do the Separation Ritual (see below).
6. Do the Cakes and Wine ritual.
7. Close the circle.
8. Finally continue to have no contact with the toxic person.

You will need your usual ritual items to cast circle and your altar. As I mentioned you will also have a length of yarn or piece of red string. The yarn/string must be long enough to encircle your own waist and to encircle the object (that represents the toxic person).

The Separation Ritual

Take the object. First, your will asperge it.

With the consecrated water, asperge and say:

I cleanse and consecrate you by water and earth.

Next you will cense the object. Cense means to waft incense smoke over the object.

With the incense smoke, cense and say:

I bless and charge you with air and fire.

Then take the string/yarn and cense and asperge it as well and say:

I cleanse and consecrate you by water and earth.

I bless and charge you with air and fire.

Take the red string/yarn in your hands saying:

Tiny bundle of String/yarn
You are now the same as the bonds between me and *Name of person.*

Tie one end of the string/yarn to the object and then encircle your waist with the other end of the string/yarn, while you say:

You are the bonds that connect us now.
From me to *Name of person* and from *Name of person* to me.
Our connection is by thee.

Sit and concentrate on the bond between you both and see it as the string/yarn that now connects you and the object. Once you have a firm connection with that thought, take the boline and cut the string/yarn, seeing in your mind's eye the astral bonds being cut along with the string/yarn.

Once you complete the cut, say:
I am now free of the ties of *Name of person* as he/she is of me.
May my happiness expand, and may *Name of person's* happiness expand.

Blessed be.

Finish up with the cakes and wine part of the ritual and then close the circle.
And you're done.

Separating ourselves from toxic people is important for our happiness and well being. It even blesses the life of the other person. You are doing yourself and the other person a favor.

I trust that this ritual will help you be happier and healthier.

Make a list of people and their limiting beliefs from which you'd like to free yourself. How will you feel when you escape the bonds of such negative beliefs and people?

_____

_____

_____

_____

_____

_____

REMOVE LIMITING BELIEFS ABOUT MONEY AND OPEN THE DOOR TO NEW PROSPERITY

In previous chapters, we've worked to remove energy blockages. Now, let's consider limiting beliefs about money that hold many people back from true abundance. These beliefs are lies you and I have learned from others. Here are examples: "You need to have money to make money." Or "Wealthy people are greedy and bad. "

Limiting beliefs cause a lot of trouble. For example, if you buy into "wealthy people are greedy and bad," you will likely, on your subconscious level, sabotage any efforts you make to create true financial abundance in your life.

In essence, you've thrown up a big brick wall that blocks the Law of Attraction from working in your favor.

Here is the good news: The meditation below will help you identify and transform these misguided beliefs into positive healthy ones.

To start with find a quiet place where you know you will not be disturbed. Turn off your phone and find a place to sit comfortably, trying to keep your back straight.

The "Release Yourself from Limiting Beliefs" Meditation

Notice now that the light begins to fade around you.

Slowly at first, it gets darker and darker.

Until you are in total darkness, were you feel safe and secure in the darkness.

(Short Pause)

Then, just as the darkness came it leaves.

The light returns, slowly at first, but gradually it gets brighter and brighter.

The light is back and you now notice you are in a new place.

You now see that you are in a great temple.

In front of you is a large stone altar, you step up to the altar.

On the altars right there is a large cauldron, and within it, there is a fire brightly burning. It is warm and soothing.

Turning back to the altar you see there three objects lying there on the smooth surface.

Each of these objects represents an untruth you have about money. They can be any belief that keeps you from prosperity.

Picking up the first object, you look closely at it.
Turn it over and around in your hands.
What untruth does this object represent?

(Pause)

Looking at your untruth you know you no longer need to hold onto this belief.
Taking the untruth, you turn to the fire on your right.
The Fire in the cauldron is warm, tossing the untruth into the fire you watch it as it is consumed by the flames. No longer to be part of your beliefs.

Picking up the second object, you look closely at it.
Turn it over and around in your hands.
What untruth does this object represent?

(Pause)

Looking at your untruth you know you no longer need to hold onto this belief either.
Taking the untruth, you turn to the fire on your right.
You toss the untruth into the fire and watch it as it is consumed by the flames. No longer to be part of your beliefs.
Now you turn to the last untruth on the altar.
Picking up this last object, you look closely at it.
Turn it over and around in your hands.

What untruth does this object represent?

(Pause)

Looking at your untruth you know you no longer need to hold onto this belief either.

Taking the untruth, you turn to the fire on your right.

You toss the untruth into the fire and watch it as it is consumed by the flames. No longer to be part of your beliefs.

You now step back from the cauldron and you notice something you didn't before. On the altar's left there is a small silver chest.

You step up to the small silver chest, as you do so you feel something in your pocket and pull it out. It is a key.

This key is the key of knowledge and truth.

You see a place to insert the key into the chest. You do so and turn the key. You hear a quiet click and the chest opens.

Inside you see three different objects representing new positive truths about money.

You pick them up.

Seeing a comfortable place to sit you take these three positive truths and sit down.

Turning each object in turn, you identify these new truths. (Pause)

You notice now that your time here is done.

You place these new objects safely into your pocket.

As you sit now you close your eyes.

Notice now that the light begins to fade around you.

Slowly at first, it gets darker and darker.

Until you are in total darkness, were you feel safe and secure in the darkness.

(Short Pause)

Then, just as the darkness came it leaves.

The light returns, slowly at first, but gradually it gets brighter and brighter.

The light is back and you now can see you are back in the room and safe.

Write down your experiences with the above meditation. What positive beliefs do you now want to hold onto and have as part of your daily living?

THE BODY AS SACRED

We've made a lot of progress in releasing blockages that stand between us and a free-flowing of the Law of Attraction in our favor. Now, it's time to tackle a big topic for many of us: How we look down upon our bodies as "imperfect. "

I'm glad to tell you that you can release a lot of heavy, painful feelings around weight and body image. Then you'll be better able to welcome the prosperity and good feelings that the Law of Attraction can provide.

When I came to the Craft, I was relieved about how Wicca viewed the body. In Wicca, it doesn't matter if you're trim or voluptuous. Or if your body has a pear shape or no shape. Wicca sees all body types as sacred. Let's face it, not everyone can be a supermodel. But just because you may not have all the "right" curves in all the right places doesn't mean you aren't beautiful in the eyes of the Gods. Because all body types are sacred to the Gods. And in Wicca, no one body type is better than another. Another thing, it doesn't matter if you're black, white, brown, or even purple. We are all beloved of the Gods.

Wiccans see the Gods in our bodies. The Gods take form in bodies just as they take form in rocks and trees around us. Because of this we need to take care of our bodies. For they are our temples. We need to feed them good food, take care of them by washing them clean, and take them out for a spin, even if it is just around the block once a day. You don't need to be a health freak to successfully maintain your body, but if you happen to be one that's okay, too. I won't tell.

Why is this so important? Healthy bodies help us do what we need to do in our magickal lives. When we take care of our bodies our bodies help us in return. Not only are they a physical manifestation of the God and Goddess, but they help us raise energy for spells. And our bodies help us interact with the world around us.

When's the last time you lit a candle without the help of your body? I'd like to light a candle with just pure thought. (It hasn't happened yet.) I need my hands to light a candle, whether I use a match or the sacred bic!

Having a healthy body is important to our magick and in honoring the Gods. As I mentioned, our body is our temple. Would you want to go to a smelly, run down and un-landscaped temple to worship in? I wouldn't want to worship there and I suspect neither would the Gods. This is why it is important to keep up your temple.

Keep your temple clean. Decorate it appropriately. For example, wear clothes that fit. You don't have to pick the latest designer clothing. Pick something you are happy with. Find your own style. You want people to see your temple and see you as the beautiful and unique person you truly are. Have an interesting body shape? Express it. Be proud of what the Gods gave you. Never hide in shame over what you look like. The Gods gave us bodies for our happiness and for enjoying the world around us.

How can you express your own style? How can you be kind to yourself and celebrate the blessing of actually having a body that works?

_____

_____

_____

_____

_____

_____

_____

_____

_____

HOW YOU CAN SUPPORT YOUR HEALTH WITH HERBS

Say you want the Law of Attraction to bring you success and financial abundance. Here's something that is apparent: Success takes energy. Without good health, one has a serious block to jumping in and taking advantage of the numerous opportunities that come when the Law of Attraction is functioning well in one's life.

A major point of this book is that the Law of Attraction can work well for you when you *remove* the blocks. Lack of health can be a major block. It can involve energy leaks related to illness. So what do you do about it?

Wiccans use herbs for all sorts of things from medicine to protection. Humans have used herbal remedies made from plants for thousands of years. Herbs comprise the oldest medicines humans have had. Many Wiccans use herbs to heal and keep themselves healthy. Being witches, we want to use nature as our healer when we get sick.

Before considering the use of herbs, heed these important considerations:

1) If you have a serious condition and/or illness, modern medicine should be used in conjunction with the old ways. For example, you shouldn't skip a trip to a medical doctor because you have heard that St. John's Wort would help with depression. Always consult with your medical doctor about herbs you're considering because some herbs may conflict with medications your doctor has prescribed or over the counter medications—or even other herbs.

2) Avoid taking an herb that you are unfamiliar with. Some herbs can be quite dangerous if used incorrectly. Certain herbs are poisonous like Belladonna. So always talk with your herbal-friendly medical doctor before taking them.

3) Some herbs you may buy at a New Age store may only be graded for magickal use. This means do NOT take such herbs internally. Be certain that the herbs you buy are food grade safe. Just because feverfew tea helps reduce a fever does NOT mean that you shouldn't use aspirin or some other modern medicine if the fever is really bad and doesn't go down. Be smart and use your head. If your affliction is serious, consult a medical doctor.

You will notice that each herb has an element, a ruling planet, and a gender. I know that the "Sun" and the "Moon" are scientifically not planets, but our ancestors didn't realize this, and so I will use the term "planet" to refer to heavenly bodies in general. The gender describes attributes the plant exhibits. Some of the male attributes are lust, sexual potency strength, and any of the more fiery properties. Some feminine properties are love, beauty, healing, and psychic powers.

The Herbs

Warning: People can discover that they are allergic to herbs that they've never used before. Be careful.

Allspice

Element: Fire
Planet: Mars
Gender: Masculine

Magickal Uses: Allspice can be easily obtained from most supermarkets or spice stores. It is a brownish powder and has a nice aromatic smell. It can be burned as an incense to attract money or luck.

Healing Uses: This herb can be used in ointments to help in healing. It can also be ingested for such purposes. Many people use it in baking today, so it is safe to ingest.

Aloe

Element: Water
Planet: The Moon
Gender: Feminine

Magickal Uses: It protects homes from accidents and protects you from evil energies.

Healing Uses: Aloe is a great healing plant, traditionally use to heal wounds. You can find this plant in many plant nurseries and stores. It has stubby green leaves with small spikes. To soothe burns, simply slice open the leaf and spread the juices on the burn site or wound area.

Apple

Element: Water
Planet: Venus
Gender: Feminine

Magickal Uses: The apple is a great choice for drawing love to you. Use the blossoms in sachets for attracting love. The flowers can be used in incense and potions. As a side note: during Samhain, Wiccans decorate their altars with one or more apples.

Healing Uses: Remember the saying an apple a day keeps the doctor away. Eating apples helps keep you healthy. Apples help regulate the digestive system. The pectin in apples provides some relief from diarrhea. Apple's high fiber helps with constipation. The leaves of the apple tree contain phloretin which acts like a natural antibiotic.

Avocado

Element: Water
Planet: Venus
Gender: Feminine

Magickal Uses: The avocado functions as an aphrodisiac. It is said that carrying an avocado pit will enhance your beauty.

Healing Uses: Research suggests that eating avocado as part of a salad allows one's body to more readily absorb fat-soluble nutrients. For example, one 2005 study demonstrated that eating avocado helped research subjects to absorb three to five times more carotenoids (antioxidant molecules). Such antioxidant molecules assist one's body to avoid free radical damage. (A "free radical" is an atom or group of atoms that has at least one unpaired electron. Such free radicals can cause damage related to cancer.)

Banana

Element: Water
Planet: Venus
Gender: Feminine

Magickal Uses: The banana is a fertility plant. It is used to cure impotency and create fertility. All parts of the banana tree are used for prosperity spells.

Healing Uses: Bananas have a high iron content and therefore help form hemoglobin in the blood, which can help anemia. Due to bananas' high potassium content, eating this fruit can help with relieving muscle cramping.

Basil

Element: Fire
Planet: Mars
Gender: Masculine

Magickal Uses: Basil is easily found at supermarkets and can be used is sachets and incense. Wiccans use basil for attracting wealth and love. Carried in a sachet, this plant can also be used for protection from negative entities. I've used basil for creating a money-drawing oil. I've also used basil as a form of incense by burning the leaves on charcoal. I felt good vibrations while doing the associated rituals.

Healing Uses: Basil is safe to eat and can be used in teas and ointments. It helps in digestion and has anti-gas properties.

Blackberry

Element: Water
Planet: Venus
Gender: Feminine

Magickal Uses: This plant provides protection, healing, and prosperity. Blackberry bushes have thorns, and this detail inspires the Wiccan belief of blackberries as a form of protection. Wiccans also use blackberry leaves in spells to acquire money.

Healing Uses: Blackberries are high in antioxidants. A number of people report that blackberry leaves relieve diarrhea. I eat blackberries as part of a healthy shake that includes raspberries, blackberries, banana, spinach, and a cup of non-fat milk.

Boneset

Element: Water
Planet: Saturn
Gender: Feminine

Magickal Uses: Wiccans use boneset to drive away evil spirits. You can make an infusion out of it and sprinkle the mixture around your living area to drive the negative entities away.

Healing Uses: Wiccans use boneset for colds and flu. They make a tea and drink it. It is also used to treat arthritis because of its anti-inflammatory properties. I feel that drinking boneset tea has helped me heal my osteoporosis to an extent.

Buchu

Element: Water
Planet: The Moon
Gender: Feminine

Magickal Uses: Some Wiccans report using buchu (also known as Agathosma betulina) in an infusion/tea to induce psychic powers and prophetic dreams.

Healing Uses: It's reported that buchu can be used for urinary tract infections and as a diuretic to help with bloating during a woman's menstrual cycle.

Buckthorn

Element: Water
Planet: Saturn
Gender: Feminine

Magickal Uses: Some Wiccans report that buckthorn can be used for protection and granting wishes. Such individuals claim that buckthorn can help in legal matters when carried or worn to court. Buckthorn is an all-around good luck bringer.

Healing Uses: Some Wiccans speak of using this herb for relieving constipation. However, be warned: This herb is strong and may cause "the runs."

Catnip

Element: Water
Planet: Venus
Gender: Feminine

Magickal Uses: This herb is great for cat magick. When used in cat spells, catnip helps you and your cat bond. It can be used in beauty and friendship spells. Catnip attracts good spirits to you when you grow it near your home.

Healing Uses: This herb when used as an infusion/tea can help relieve indigestion and heartburn. Some Wiccans use catnip as a slight sedative for humans. It works great as a relaxing tea before bed.

Cedar

Element: Fire
Planet: The Sun
Gender: Masculine

Magickal Uses: Cedar when burned is an effective herb for purification. It is also a great choice in protection from evil.

Healing Uses: It is good at repelling pests, especially of the moth variety.

Celery

Element: Fire
Planet: Mercury
Gender: Masculine

Magickal Uses: Chewing the seeds is said to help with concentration. Wiccans also use celery seeds in dream pillows to promote sleep.

Healing Uses: Some Wiccans report that celery extract helps relieve gout. In Chinese medicine, celery is sometimes used to treat high blood pressure. It has been said that celery seeds reduce blood sugar levels, which would help diabetics.

Chamomile

Element: Water
Planet: The Sun
Gender: Masculine

Magickal Uses: Used to fight curses and spells. It is also a great herb to attract money.

Healing Uses: Wiccans use chamomile to support sleep. It's said to reduce anxiety and stress.

Cinnamon

Element: Fire
Planet: The Sun
Gender: Masculine

Magickal Uses: It is used for success, psychic powers, lust, and love spells. It can be burned as incense to attract money and to bring back health.

Healing Uses: Some research studies suggest that cinnamon helps in cases of high blood glucose levels.

Dill

Element: Fire
Planet: Mercury
Gender: Masculine

Magickal Uses: Dill can be used for protection when hung in the home or carried in a purse. Placing this herb over a doorway is said to block negative influences from entering. Because it has a large number of seeds, dill is often used in money and prosperity spells.

Healing Uses: Besides being a great preservative, dill helps in other ways. It helps the digestive tract by relaxing the muscles in your digestive system, and it also helps urinary tract infections. It does this by inhibiting the bacteria that cause bladder infections.

Dragon's Blood

Element: Fire
Planet: Mars
Gender: Masculine

Magickal Uses: Some Wiccans use dragon's blood for protection and exorcism. This is a great herb to use in incense to boost your spell's power.

Healing Uses: Some consider dragon's blood as a food preservative because of its high phenolic content. Warning: It is dangerous to use dragon's blood because merely getting the oil on one's skin causes bruising.

Eucalyptus

Element: Water
Planet: Moon
Gender: Feminine

Magickal Uses: Eucalyptus leaves and pods can be carried for protection. Wiccans sometimes stuff a healing poppet with eucalyptus leaves. (See the section following herbs for more information on poppets.)

Healing Uses: Eucalyptus loosens phlegm and helps you cough the goop up. It has antibacterial properties, and it helps heal minor scrapes and cuts.

Fennel

Element: Fire
Planet: Mercury
Gender: Masculine

Magickal Uses: Wiccans use fennel to ward off evil spirits. You can grow fennel in containers in various spots in the home. You may also hang fennel by windows and doors.

Healing Uses: Fennel is said to promote the production of bile. Either chewing the seeds or making a tea out of fennel helps the digestive tract.

Feverfew

Element: Water
Planet: Venus
Gender: Masculine

Magickal Uses: When carried, feverfew protects you from accidents, colds, and fevers.

Healing Uses: Some Wiccans consider feverfew tea to be great at reducing fevers.

Flax

Element: Fire
Planet: Mercury
Gender: Masculine
Magickal Uses: Flax is used to ward off poverty and to increase prosperity. You use it by placing some flax seeds in

your purse or wallet.

Healing Uses: When eaten, flax can reduce cholesterol because it is high in fiber. Because of its high fiber content, flax can reduce blood sugar levels.

Frankincense

Element: Fire
Planet: The Sun
Gender: Masculine

Magickal Uses: Wiccans use frankincense for protection from evil and exorcising evil. Some Wiccans burn frankincense to induce visions to assist with their personal growth.

Healing Uses: A number of people use frankincense to promote healing and to prevent scarring left by wounds.

Garlic

Element: Fire
Planet: Mars
Gender: Masculine

Magickal Uses: Wiccans use garlic for healing and protection. A number of individuals use garlic as an anti-theft herb. It is said to keep "sticky fingers away."

Healing Uses: Garlic has antibacterial properties. For this reason, garlic is useful for some skin rashes.

Ginger

Element: Fire
Planet: Mars
Gender: Masculine

Magickal Uses: It is said that eating ginger before doing your magick spells helps increase your power. Ginger is often used in love spells, too. Ginger root can be ground up and sprinkled in your pocket or purse/wallet to increase prosperity.

Healing Uses: This herb is used as a anti-nausea medicine for motion sickness and morning sickness.

Ginseng

Element: Fire
Planet: The Sun
Gender: Masculine

Magickal Uses: Wiccans use ginseng in love, beauty, protection, and lust spells. You can carry a ginseng root to attract love and also to guard your health.

Healing Uses: Ginseng is known for enhancing the immune system. Warning: It is reported that some people experience insomnia, menstrual problems, increased heart rate, high or low blood pressure, or other side effects.

Hibiscus

Element: Water
Planet: Venus
Gender: Feminine

Magickal Uses: Wiccans use the blossoms in love incenses for spells and in sachets.

Healing Uses: It is said that drinking hibiscus tea daily lowers high blood pressure. Researchers state that more studies are needed to verify this suggestion.

Hops

Element: Air
Planet: Mercury
Gender: Masculine

Magickal Uses: Wiccans include hop in protection charms. They sometimes scatter hops on a floor and use it during an exorcism ritual.

Healing Uses: It is controversial as to how hops serve for medicinal purposes. Some homeopathic practitioners suggest that hops serve to calm and relieve muscle spasms.

Juniper

Element: Fire
Planet: The Sun
Gender: Masculine

Magickal Uses: Some Wiccans use juniper for protection against evil forces, theft, accidents, and wild animal attacks.

Healing Uses: Some individuals use it in certain forms to help one breathe more freely. Some people find juniper similar to pepper for increasing circulation.

Lavender

Element: Air
Planet: Mercury
Gender: Masculine

Magickal Uses: Lavender is used in love sachets and for purification baths. Many use lavender as part of aroma therapy in that it promotes peace and happiness.

Healing Uses: Lavender can be used for reducing anxiety and stress. I have incorporated lavender in my personal, homemade hand balm. I find it calming. It helps me relax and sleep well. I have a friend who has used lavender oil for poison ivy. It helps relieve the itch and helps dry up the lesions. Its smell, though not unpleasant, is very intense, so she never used it at work, only at home.

Licorice

Element: Water
Planet: Venus
Gender: Feminine

Magickal Uses: Chewing on licorice (not the candy) can aid in love spells and is often used in sachets for such purposes.

Healing Uses: Some Wiccans use licorice as a cough remedy and for relieving sore throats.

Myrrh

Element: Water
Planet: The Moon
Gender: Feminine

Magickal Uses: Wiccans burn myrrh to purify an area. Myrrh helps boost the power of other incenses, and it is often incorporated in the manufacture of a number of incense sticks.

Healing Uses: Myrrh fights bacteria. Ancient Egyptians used myrrh as a mouthwash.

Passion Flower

Element: Water
Planet: Venus
Gender: Feminine

Magickal Uses: When placed in the home, passion flower promotes peace. Passion flower in the bedroom makes it easier to fall asleep.

Healing Uses: Passion flower is used to combat stress, anxiety, and insomnia.

Pomegranate

Element: Fire
Planet: Mercury
Gender: Masculine

Magickal Uses: Eating the seeds helps increase fertility. Use the dried skin of the pomegranate in money spells of all kinds.

All these herbs can be used for body and mind. What herbs do you think can benefit you? (Warning: Get sound medical advice and be careful when interacting with herbs that are new to you.)

THE QUICK MOOD PICK-ME-UPS

Moods can help you or hold you back. Ever feel fully-energized? Did you get a lot done? To say it simply, a good mood can help you attract more opportunities and throw wide the door for the Law of Attraction to flow well in your life.

On the other hand, a low mood can shut you down. With no action, you could actually miss out on the opportunities that the Law of Attraction is trying to deliver to you.

So it's better to become skilled with improving your moods when possible.

A short time before a 4th of July fireworks display was set to start, I sat in a field watching children running, jumping and playing nearby. Their joyful shouts rang in my ears. And an idea arose in my thoughts: I wish I could just let go like these children and be free from the drudgery of life.

We all have our moments of sadness, some more than

others. Oh to be carefree and happy like a child!

So I came up with the *Quick Mood Pick-me-up for Wiccans.* As some of you may know, I battle depression everyday and these methods can be a lifesaver when in a downer mood. It may not make you as perky and carefree as a happy child, but it will certainly move your mood in a better direction to help you get out of a low mood.

Here are The Quick Mood Pick-me-up for Wiccans methods:

• Lay down in a field of living grass

Laying in grass is relaxing. Further, it's easier for some people to let go when they have more bodily contact with the earth. The process is simple:

Concentrate on the ground beneath you.

Let any negative energy flow from you into the ground. Imagine the ground is a sponge, sucking the negative energy from your body and cleansing the body.

Take deep breaths and let your body relax.

Let Goddess take away all your worries and fears.

• Light a candle

If you have racing thoughts, simply light a candle and concentrate on the flame. This can ease your mind.

Cast a circle and place the candle in front of you. You can bless and consecrate it. Make your ritual as simple or as elaborate as you prefer.

Relax and watch the flame.

Breathe slowly and imagine sending your thoughts into the flame to be cleansed from your mind. In this way, you empty your mind of your troubled thoughts.

• Hug a tree

I know this must sound a little silly, but hugging a tree is a great way to shunt negative energy into the earth. Any tree will gladly help you.
Wrap your arms around the tree.

Take three deep breaths in and let the tree absorb your negative energy. The tree will do the rest.

Trees naturally shunt energy into the earth. This makes them a great resource for our imbalances in life.

• Take a walk in the woods

This is one of the easier practices and it's great exercise. Remember what I shared about trees. In fact just being around trees (and nature) reduces stress. Fear not city dwellers, a park will work just as well. Take deep breaths and relax. Look at your surroundings and see the Gods in all the flowers and trees. Know that you are not alone in your walk, for the Gods walk with you. They support us when no one else can–and even at those times when you might not believe in yourself. The Gods want the best for you.

• Talk to a friend

Some people find that they allow being busy to deprive them of actually talking with a friend. Don't let that happen.

Talk with a friend and often things appear clearer. Expressing yourself can wash away the stress and pain of the drudgery of day to day living. If you have a High Priest or Priestess talk to him or her. They are there to support you in your journey. This can be a great bonding experience for both of you.

So if you find yourself in a low mood, remember the Quick Mood Pick-me-up for Wiccans methods. I hope they help you as much as they help me.

Which Quick Mood Pick-me-ups do you want to implement in your life? What times during your day will you make the methods work for you?

_____

_____

_____

_____

_____

_____

_____

_____

HOW TO RELEASE YOURSELF
FROM SELF-JUDGMENT

Self-judgment can be a huge barrier or block between you and the power of the Law of Attraction. Why? If you judge yourself harshly, you'll probably emotionally shutdown. Then nothing gets done. You don't make the phone calls; you don't write the emails. You don't make the contacts.

Fortunately, you can release yourself from self-judgment and restore the positive flow of opportunity in your life.

As an example, I'll share my personal story:

I never expected to be a writer, but the Gods visited me in a dream. I have dyslexia: Writing was the furthest thing from my imagination. In fact, my degrees are in art and web/graphic design.

But the Gods gave me a task: Write a book for beginners of the Craft that is straightforward and easy to read.

When I awoke, I felt excited but scared about how I could

possibly accomplish this book-writing task. I knew the demands of writing a book because I have close friends who are writers.

How could I possibly write enough to fill a whole book?! It was agony to merely read the first book in the *Harry Potter* series due to my dyslexia.

I started to compare myself to other writers by thinking "I'm not a Scott Cunningham or a Starhawk. What am I to do?

I kept thinking about all the other writers of books I had slowly read. Their books were so good. I couldn't match that. The anxiety grabbed me in the chest and I had trouble breathing.

But I strongly believe in the Gods. I know the Gods would not set me up to fail. They love me, and if they say I can do it, I can.

The hardest part for me wasn't the task itself, but the constant comparing that I did, placing myself against other writers.

With all of my misspellings, I took blows to my self-esteem each day. My mind raced with negative thoughts of no one will care about what I have to say; no will read it, and this will never help anyone.

With all this negativity in my mind, it's a miracle I got anything done. I slowly began to realize something. I cannot compare myself to anyone else. Why? The book I'm writing is a snapshot in time of me. It's about my truth. No one can write it for me.

I was so busy comparing myself to others when in reality there is no comparison. There can't be. I am me, no one else, and all those racing thoughts were not true.

• Someone will read my book (my editors, for example)

• People will be able to easily read it because my editors will smooth out any rough sections (I love my editors!)

• Someone cares about what I have to say (that someone is me!)

My book has already helped someone, me.

My book taught me a valuable lesson: Don't judge or compare yourself to others.

We all have gifts, different levels of ability. These combinations make us unique and strong. No one else has our particular knowledge and unique set of talents, and this makes each of us special.

Comparing my special to your special cannot be done. It's like comparing strawberries and octopi. Because our experiences in life are all slightly or dramatically different (as in different cultures). You just can't compare the two. They are not the same.

All I need to do is remember strawberries and octopi.

You're special. Drop comparing yourself to others.
Bring your own special gifts to bear.

The Gods love you and enjoy when you express your
creativity.

**How can you express your creativity? How can you get
support so you can continue to explore and find new ways
to express yourself?**

_____

_____

_____

_____

_____

_____

_____

_____

THE ALTAR

In previous chapters, we have learned to release blocks. We also practiced grounding to release unwanted energy in our lives. A number of readers have likely tried meditation by this point.

The above methods help us to create sacred space in our minds. Now, we'll make sacred space around us in the physical world. We will start this process with creating an altar. Think of it as your work desk in creating an abundant life.

When I first started learning about altar setups, it took me a long time to remember where everything should be placed. I felt self conscious about making mistakes. My mentor would simply smile at me and move the item I had misplaced to where it should reside on the altar.

My point is: do not beat yourself up if you get it wrong. Note that there are many ways to set up an altar, and each person or group has a specific method. This chapter shows you an example of a typical altar setup.

What's on an altar? Let's start with the upper right side of the table and move around clockwise.

1) Cakes/Bread: It is acceptable to use bread, cupcakes, cookies, or even a power bar. It should contain carbohydrates to nourish the body and replenish the energy you use during the ritual.

2) Censer & Incense: In this case, the incense burner holds cone incense. However, it is acceptable to burn any kind of incense you choose. Remember that incense, when burned, represents Air on your altar.

3) Taper: The taper is for lighting candles. You begin by using a lighter to ignite the wick of the working candle. Then, you bring the taper to the working candle and ignite the wick of the taper. Now with the lit taper you ignite the other candles on your altar.

4) Lighter: The lighter is used to light the working candle. Any type of lighter may be used.

5) Bell/Chime: A bell or chime is needed for different purposes during a ritual.

6) Pentacle: The pentacle is used to help focus your attention on your goal.

7) Athame: The athame knife is used to direct power and for casting circles.
8) Bowl with Water: Water is one of the five elements. It is

used together with salt to make consecrated water.

9) Dish with Salt: Salt represents the Earth. It is placed into water to make consecrated water.

10) Chalice with Wine: As you remember, the cup is a female symbol. In a ritual, the cup holds the wine or juice that is to be blessed. (It is acceptable to use juice instead of wine if you do not drink alcohol.)

11) Offering Dishes: These dishes are used to "offer up," as an offering, part of your blessed food from your "cakes and wine" ceremony. We will discuss that later. You can also offer up flowers, which pay tribute to nature and the Goddess.

12) Goddess Candle & God Candle: These are the candles that represent the God and Goddess.

13) Working Candle: The working candle is positioned between the God and Goddess candle. Use this candle to light the other candles during a ritual. The working candle represents the element Fire on your altar.

You will find that, with a little practice, setting up your altar will become second nature to you.

Notice that I do not include the besom, or broom, because it is a tool that is not always used.

The basic setup listed here will get you started doing rituals. The tools need not cost you a lot of money. At first, I found many of my tools in secondhand stores. You can also use antiques or the latest designs from your local artists. The choice is yours.

You must be wary of secondhand items that may contain negative energy. Pick out tools that feel right to you. If one doesn't feel right, then don't use it.

Simple Cleansing and Dedication Ritual for Your Tools

In this section, we will explore a simple ritual to cleanse and dedicate your tools.

First, realize that cleansing and dedication steps are best done before you use your tools. The process only needs to be done once.

If you want to cast a circle and you have not consecrated your athame yet, you can cast a circle using your finger like an athame. Once you have cast the circle and have done a cleansing ritual on the athame, then you can cleanse the rest of your tools with the consecrated athame.

1) Cast your circle (details found later in this book).
2) Pick up the tool (an athame, wand, chalice, or whatever you are cleansing) to be dedicated. Sprinkle the consecrated water you made on the tool. Say:

I exorcise thee, o (name of tool), that I cleanse and consecrate you with Earth and Water.

3) Place the consecrated water down.

4) Take the tool and place it over the burning incense and let the smoke from the incense waft over the tool. Say:

I charge and bless you with Fire and Air, and I here do dedicate this (name of tool) in the names of the Goddess and the God.

5) Now you can do the cakes and wine ceremony.

6) Lastly, close the circle.

That's it. You're done!

* * *

This chapter has revealed the items needed for your altar. As I mentioned, with practice, you'll be able to set up your altar with ease.

How can you create an altar of your own? How would you customize your own sacred space?

_____

_____

_____

_____

_____

OVERCOME MISINFORMATION ABOUT MAGICK

Magick is a natural power, not a supernatural one. When we do magick, we channel natural energies and create change with them.

As I mentioned earlier, I believe that the Law of Attraction is actually magick. The problem is that many people do not have the rest of the story. This book has been designed to give you such information.

Let's continue with magick as a natural power. If Wicca isn't really supernatural, then why practice Wicca at all? Why not follow another spiritual path? It would certainly be easier to go with a mainstream religion. You wouldn't get the dirty looks and troublesome accusations that are so often directed at Wiccans. Why practice any religion for that matter?

Everyone is different and has their own answer to that

question. I like to think of religion as a bottle of wine. Let's say you have three different people who all taste the same bottle of wine. The first person points out that the flavor has accents of oak. The second praises the hints of apple in it, and the third enjoys the floral notes. They are all right. The wine contains all the flavors they described. But each person detected something different. Religion is like that. Deity can't be entirely known. So the truth of it is scattered into many faiths.

I love nature, and I enjoy these "notes" of the wine. The beauties and wonders of nature surround me. Other paths require that you must go somewhere to be with Deity—a mosque, a church, or another particular place where you go to God. This doesn't work for me.

On the other hand, with Wicca, the Gods are not only everywhere and all around me at all times, but they are within me as well. I am never without my Gods. And they come to circle often when asked.

That's right, your eyes didn't deceive you in that last paragraph. I am literally the Goddess and God, and these Gods don't judge me! They support me, love me, and help me just for who I am, not for what I look like. I don't need to change or alter myself to be loved. No diets or creams are required. The best thing about all this spiritual yumminess is that it's all part of the natural world. That's the thing I love most. The Gods are of the trees, the birds, the stag, the Earth itself.

The natural world is what I live in, and it is my reality. I'm not trying to get to some euphoric place I've never experienced. I'm not trying to jump impossible hurdles with rules that can never truly be successfully followed. All I must do is be me. That's it.

We are rewarded with love and kindness when we give love and kindness. What we put out into the universe, the universe gives us back threefold. This cycle, among all the others, is all natural. Angry, vengeful god, not included! And that's the way I like it.

How do you already see magick in your life everyday? How can you support yourself and make space for you to practice magick and the Law of Attraction?

_____

_____

_____

_____

_____

_____

_____

CASTING A CIRCLE OF SACRED SPACE

Earlier, I mentioned that your altar is your work desk. Also, I noted that, to me, the Law of Attraction is magick and that we just need more information about how to make such magick work well. Now, we'll cover how to create the sacred workspace around the altar.

To practice magick, Wiccans use tools, altars, grounding exercises, and the practice of raising power or energy. Rituals combine all of these pieces into one harmonious rite. The casting of a circle is where it all comes together.

When first casting circles, I felt nervous about making a mistake. I cast my first circles when I was a solitary witch. Soon I gained some confidence while becoming more and more familiar with the process.

The casting circle is valuable because it's where your ritual work is practiced. The casting circle functions as the doorway between the worlds, both the mundane world and the spirit world. When you cast a circle, you create a temple of energy. This temple or circle is where you worship the Gods and Goddesses and work magick. The circle contains the energy raised by the practitioner(s) and prevents the energy's dissipation until it has been used. It also keeps out unwanted entities and, due to its sacred nature, aids the ritual work.

Casting a circle involves several steps. The following lays this out for you in detail.

Setup

Before you begin, you will need:

1) A table for the altar.
2) Candles and candleholders for the four directions in the colors that represent each (red for south, blue for west, green for north, yellow for east.)
3) A red candle for the God and a green candle for the Goddess. These candle colors are preferable but not mandatory. You may also use white candles, which represent all colors.
4) A working candle to represent the element Fire.
5) A cup or chalice.
6) An athame.
7) A sword. If you don't have one, use the athame to cast the circle.
8) Incense and incense burner.
9) A dish of salt, preferably sea salt.
10) A bowl of water.
11) A bell or chime.
12) An altar cloth to keep wax and the other things off the table.

13) Wine or juice and some sort of cake.

14) A lighter.

15) A taper (to light the other candles from the working candle).

Next, locate the four directions (north, south, east and west); you can use a compass. Wiccans divide the area of the circle into four parts ("quarters"), corresponding with the four directions. Place the "quarter candles" in their respective corners: green in the northern-most corner, yellow in the east, red in the south, and blue in the west.

The Script

Before you begin, ground and center using the Tree of Life meditation exercise (found earlier in this book). This will help to clean out and balance your energy. This vital step helps you get into the right frame of mind before you start.

Next, you need a script to cast a circle or temple for conducting harmonious rites. Don't worry if the rites you perform don't flow easily at first. You just need practice. Consider writing your own script to follow. This may make it less confusing for you.

The following is an example of a script you can use. The parts you say out loud are in bold. This makes it easier to be seen by candlelight.

Note: This script is written for someone who is casting alone.

1) Knock three times on the altar. Ring the bell three times.

2) Light the working candle with the lighter and put it down on the altar. (The other candles will be lit later using the taper.)

3) Light the charcoal (if you are using it) from the working candle. (The incense will placed on the charcoal later.)

4) Take your athame and place its tip into the flame of the working candle. Say:

I exorcise* you o creature of fire. And I consecrate and bless you in the names of the Goddess and the God that you are pure and clean.

(*Note: When we speak of exorcise here, we are purifying the item by driving out any negative energies.)

5) Trace a pentacle (a five-pointed star) over the flame. Pick up the candle and raise it up above you and imagine the Gods' energy filling the flame. Place the candle back on the altar.

6) Take your athame and place its tip into the bowl of water. Say:

I exorcise you, o creature of water. And I consecrate and bless you in the names of the Goddess and the God that you are pure and clean.

7) Trace a pentacle in the water. Pick up the bowl of water

and raise it up above you and imagine your energy and the Gods' energy filling the water. Place the bowl back on the altar.

8) Take your athame and place its tip into the salt. Say:

I exorcise you, o creature of salt. And I consecrate and bless you in the names of the Goddess and the God that you are pure and clean.

9) Trace a pentacle in the salt. Pick up the bowl of salt and raise it up above you and imagine your energy and the Gods' energy filling the salt. Place the salt bowl back on the altar.

10) Take your athame and place its tip into the incense. Say:

I exorcise you, o creature of Air. And I consecrate and bless you in the names of the Goddess and the God that you are pure and clean.

11) Trace a pentacle over incense. Pick up the incense and raise it up above you and imagine your energy and the Gods' energy filling the incense. Place the incense on the lit charcoal.

12) Take your athame and scoop up three blades of the salt. You may also use your finger. Put the three pinches of salt into the water and mix it with the blade of your athame to make consecrated water. Pick up the bowl of consecrated water and raise it up above you and imagine your energy and the Gods' energy filling it.

13) Take the consecrated water (the salt and water mixture) and dip your fingers into it. Dab some of it on your inner wrists and forehead. Say:

I bless myself with Earth and Water.

14) Take the censer filled with the burning incense and wave the smoke over you. Say:

I bless myself with Air and Fire.

15) Take the consecrated water and use your fingers to asperge (sprinkle with consecrated water) the circle. Starting with north and moving clockwise, walk a complete circle around the perimeter, aspersing each corner as you go. When finished, place the bowl back on the altar.

16) Pick up the censer filled with the burning incense. Use your hand to wave the incense smoke around the circle. Starting with north and moving clockwise, walk a complete circle around the perimeter, waving the smoke as you go. Be careful not to burn yourself or anything else. When finished, place the censer back on the altar.

You have just cleansed the space and yourself. Now let's continue by casting the circle.

17) Take the athame. Envision energy being channeled from you and coming out the tip of your athame [You point the athame outward, away from you as you create the circle.] Starting with north and moving clockwise, walk a complete circle around the perimeter. As you walk, say:

I conjure you, o circle of power, that you be a boundary between the seen mundane world and the spirit world, that you protect me and contain the magick that I shall raise within you! I consecrate and bless you in the names of the Goddess and the God. So mote it be!

18) Finish at the east quarter (direction).
Now it's time to "call the quarters." (This refers to the four directions.)

19) Pick up the athame and the taper from the altar. Light the taper from the working candle. Go and stand in the east corner of where your circle boundary is. Starting with the east candle, say:

I summon, stir, and call you up, o mighty ones of the East, element of Air. Come guard my circle and witness my rite.

20) Trace a pentacle in the air with your athame. Then light the quarter candle for east. Say:

Hail and welcome!

21) Move clockwise to the south candle. Say:

I summon, stir, and call you up, o mighty ones of the South, element of Fire. Come guard my circle and witness my rite.

22) Trace a pentacle in the air with your athame. Then light the quarter candle for south. Say:

Hail and welcome!

23) Move clockwise to the west candle. Say:

I summon, stir, and call you up, o mighty ones of the West, element of Water. Come guard my circle and witness my rite.

24) Trace a pentacle in the air with your athame. Then light the quarter candle for west. Say:

Hail and welcome!

25) Move clockwise to the north candle. Say:

I summon, stir, and call you up, o mighty ones of the North, element of Earth. Come guard my circle and witness my rite.

26) Trace a pentacle in the air with your athame. Then light the quarter candle for north. Say:

Hail and welcome!

27) Return to the altar. Using the taper, light the Goddess candle, saying:

Welcome, my Lady!

28) Using the taper, light the God candle, saying:

Welcome, my Lord!

You have now completed casting your circle!

At this time you can do any working or communicate with the Gods through meditation.

Cakes and Wine Ceremony

As a form of magick, the Law of Attraction requires that you keep yourself in empowered state.

After any ritual, it is important to replenish and ground your energy. Food and drink help to replenish the energy spent doing the working or ritual. Food also helps you to ground.

But first you must bless the sustenance. Begin with the wine or juice.

1) Take the cup from your altar and pour the wine or juice into it. Then take the athame and dip its tip into the wine or juice. Say:

As the athame is to the male, so the cup is to the female, and so joined bring union and harmony.

2) Pour some of your blessed wine or juice into the offering bowl or plate on your altar. Say:

To the Gods!

You can now partake of the beverage.

3) Take your athame and point it over the cake. Say:

Blessed be these cakes that they bestow health, peace, joy, strength, and that fulfillment of love that is perpetual

happiness.

4) Take one of the cakes (or just a piece) and place it in the offering bowl or plate. Say:

To the Gods!

You can now partake of the blessed cakes.

Note that this ritual was written for someone practicing alone. If it is conducted in a group, pass around the cup and the cakes, each person taking a sip and one of or part of the cake. As each person passes the wine and cake, this is the process:

As you hand the cup to another, say: **May you never thirst.**

The other person replies: **Blessed Be.**

As you offer a cake, say: **May you never hunger.**

The other person replies: **Blessed Be.**

After everyone has had some cake and wine (or juice) in this part of the ceremony, ask for feedback from the group about how the ritual went. You can now talk about experiences you had during the ritual or bring up feedback about the ritual. Relax and enjoy the rest of the food and drink, which will ground and replenish your spent energies.

So, what do you do with the blessed offerings in the offering dishes? You certainly don't just throw it into the garbage! They are gifts to the Gods. Take them outside to your garden where you can leave it on the ground to help nourish the Earth.

If you do not have a garden at your home, you can take the offerings out into the woods and leave them there. Some Wiccans who live in the city set the blessed offering out on their porch for local animals to partake. Be sure to only leave biodegradable food. Avoid wrappers or containers that will not decompose.

Closing Your Circle

It is very important to dismiss the energies you have called for your circle. Be sure to take down the magick temple (circle) you erected. And certainly dismiss the quarters!

If you forget to do these crucial steps, mishaps are sure to happen. It would be like telling the Elementals, "Make yourselves at home!" And they will. Elementals are not bad or evil; it's just that they can be mischievous. Fire Elementals will start fires! Water Elementals might mess with your plumbing. They don't act out of malice, but causing problems seems to be in their nature. They are great allies when practicing magick, but they need to go home when you are done. So please remember to dismiss them.

To close your circle:

1) Take your athame and hold it up and stand facing the east. Say:

Hail mighty ones of the East, the element of Air. I thank you for guarding my circle and witnessing my rite. May

you depart to your fair and lovely realms. I bid you hail and farewell!

2) Trace a pentacle in the air with your athame.

3) Continuing, moving in a clockwise circle, stand facing the south. Say:

Hail mighty ones of the South, the element of Fire. I thank you for guarding my circle and witnessing my rite. May you depart to your fair and lovely realms. I bid you hail and farewell!

4) Trace a pentacle in the air with your athame.

5) Moving clockwise around the circle, stand facing west. Say:

Hail mighty ones of the West, the element of Water. I thank you for guarding my circle and witnessing my rite. May you depart to your fair and lovely realms. I bid you hail and farewell!

6) Trace a pentacle in the air with your athame.

7) Moving clockwise around the circle, stand facing north. Say:

Hail mighty ones of the North, the element of Earth. I thank you for guarding my circle and witnessing my rite. May you depart to your fair and lovely realms. I bid you hail and farewell!

8) Trace a pentacle in the air with your athame.

9) Return again to face east. While walking the boundary of the circle, say:

Fire seal the circle round,
Let it fade beneath the ground,
Let all things be as they once were before.
The circle is now no more,
Merry meet, merry part,
And merry meet again!
So mote it be!

Generally, the above is how to close a circle. However, each coven or practitioner may have slightly different variations on wording. Yet the process remains the same.

How do you feel about creating your own sacred space? Where in your home can you set up your own sacred space?

_____

_____

_____

_____

_____

_____

_____

_____

_____

HOW TO DO A PROSPERITY SPELL

Many of us come to the Law of Attraction out of a sincere desire to increase financial abundance in our lives.

Money Magick

"If you're a Wiccan and magick is real, why aren't you rich?" A simple, but valid question. So why are many Wiccans and magickal people in general struggling so much with money? One answer is: Many of us see a focus on money as un-spiritual. We do not see it as part of a spiritual path.

Have you noticed that many of us struggle for our daily needs of food on the table and a roof over our heads? Priests and priestesses focus on helping others. But many ignore money until they're struggling. Then money, or really the lack of money, monopolizes their attention. When that happens, they cannot help others. Having money, while not the most important thing in life, is valuable—like oxygen.

Being wealthy not only serves us in the materialistic world, but creates spiritual well being. How? Wealth, or abundance, creates a peaceful space in which you can breathe easy and even help others. With this understanding, it's truly helpful to incorporate money into our spiritual practice.

Here is a powerful idea: using magick to help us gain wealth assists us to fulfill our spiritual needs. Again, I am talking about abundance. When you experience abundance and take care of your financial needs, you do something truly valuable: you remove the distress that many people feel about money. Such distress is so distracting that it takes up too much energy and can make people feel miserable. Wouldn't it be better to have your financial needs fulfilled and to even have an abundance of financial and other blessings? Why? Because you can share with others from a place of personal strength and wholeness.

An important note: let's focus on the idea that we're encouraged to do what is necessary to create financial abundance on the physical plane. Many Wiccans have regular jobs or serve others through their efforts as business owners. You do not have to use magick to gain money and financial abundance.

Here's another way to look at it. You can eat a healthy diet for your physical health. You may not absolutely need vitamin supplements. But why take a chance? Personally, I eat well and take vitamins. Don't you?

Similarly, you could try to keep your job and other money-generating activities separate from your spiritual life.

But why not incorporate how you serve others (that's what you're doing when you work in your own business or for an employer) into your spiritual life?

Doesn't it make sense to develop a spiritual life that includes abundance and wealth? By the way, I notice that some Wiccans feel more comfortable about doing a spell for "transportation" which provides for the possibility that one gets a pass for using public transportation or that a relative gives a castoff old car. That is fine. We can ask whether it's okay to also have more options that money can provide.

You notice I used the word wealthy earlier and not "rich." I purposely use the word "wealthy." So what's the difference? Rich is the flow of money coming in; wealth is a state of having money. I think author Jason Miller says it well:

A rich person has a high income, which is a stream that can feed being wealthy or being in debt, depending on how that money is used. There is no shortage of people with high incomes but no real wealth. . . . Wealth is not a flow of income; it is a state of positive finances.

I've talked with some Wiccans who say that when money is tight, they use magick to pay the rent or a credit card bill. And this works. However, too often we ask magick to fix our problems when these difficulties have grown too large. We wait until we have no other option than to use our magick. We come from a place of desperation instead of a place of balance.

Again, I want to share that it's healthier to take care of

money-related concerns so that you do not "just get by." Instead, you do what is necessary to enjoy abundance and balance. Ideally, Wiccans use magick to get to an inner state where they work out problems that prevent them from enjoying such abundance. For example, some Wiccans may do many prosperity spells but perhaps, would benefit more for a healing spell so that they learn to save money and improve their spending habits.

The first step for using magick effectively for financial well-being is to work our magick in a consistent manner not only to sustain us but also to build something more out of our money.

Too often we use magick to maintain where we are at, and we don't use magick to build us up to where we want to go.

So it seems practical to use magick to create sustained wealth. The question is: What can magick do, and what can't it do? Jason Miller suggests, "Practical magic can do two things: it can affect the minds of other people; and it can shift probability in your favor, making improbable things more probable."

This sounds good. However, we must take care and remember The Law of Three—what you send out returns to you with three times the force. Remember, messing with someone's free will is simply wrong, and it will likely cause havoc in your life.

So what is the proper use of magick? It is a measured use. For example, for a job interview, you can devise a spell that includes the words: "May I be at my best during my interview. May the interviewer be feeling well during our time together. May the interview turn out for the good of all involved."

Do you notice how you are not trying to force the situation and push the interviewer to hire you, even if you are not the ideal candidate in their mind? The Gods may see that this job is not ideal for you, and you may not be seeing it.

Your spell does not conflict with the Gods protecting you from an inappropriate employment situation.

Get Clear About Wealth

It's reported that Buckminster Fuller said the wealth can be measured in the number of days that one can live one's normal lifestyle without a paycheck.

So it's not the amount that comes in that is the key; it's how much you keep and use to build your abundant finances. We're not talking about becoming misers. Money needs to flow in order to work. Think of it like water: it needs to flow and move, or it gets stagnant and bad. Money needs to flow in cycles. Author Larry Winget said, "When you share what you have earned with others, then it magically comes back to you. I don't know why it works, but it works."

So having wealth is what we need, not just being rich. And to experience true wealth, we have money flow in our lives like water. This is where magick comes in.

Let's focus on avoiding the big mistake—using spells the wrong way, that is, doing spells and magick only when we are desperate for money.

Instead, create a healthy relationship with money. A healthy relationship is not one in which a partner only comes to the other person during times of desperation. You build the relationship day by day and year by year.

On the other hand, here is an example of taking a desperate approach toward increasing one's income. One year, I sought to increase my abundance. I, like many others, only asked for financial help when I was in trouble. I would do a spell here and there, seeking a windfall or at least something to get me by.

With this mentality, most of my money spells at that time would fail. Once it even backfired on me. I had done an elaborate spell to seek help for improving my finances. It was the same month that a large portion of my income suddenly dried up. It felt like my magick had turned against me.

I thought long and hard about it. Slowly I began to realize my mistake. I needed wealth not "quick money." So I did a different spell. Instead of asking for prosperity to simply drop into my lap, I asked that it be returned to me in whatever legal means possible and that I have the energy to accomplish the necessary actions to bring in income.

So I did a spell to ask for the strength and energy that I needed to create my own financial wealth. I realized that I was my own source of energy and that I was the one to create the money I desired. As I continued doing spells toward my goal, I didn't concentrate on the money aspect of it. I concentrated on the end result. I concentrated on how I could build on what I did have to create wealth in my life.

This is what happened. Every week I would honor the Gods with an offering of incense or by burning a candle to them. I thanked them for their guidance in this new endeavor and for helping to build my capabilities to accomplish my goal of wealth. I did another spell, keeping in mind my goal, and I continued to burn offerings to the Gods.

Several weeks went by. Then one night I awoke with a wild idea: I needed to write a book. So the next day when I got up, I could hardly contain all the excitement and energy I had for the plan. I had even dreamt up a title in my sleep. I checked online to see if it was available, and it was. I knew then that the Gods were guiding me, and this was what they wanted for me. My first step was to begin a blog. My initial concern was that my dyslexia would hinder my attempt to write. I figured that writing a blog would help get my feet wet. So I started www.TheHiddenChildrenoftheGoddess.com.

I now know that I will be just fine. I know that my writing will help others as well as myself. When you write a book, you naturally dig deeper and learn during your journey of writing. And the book I was guided to write is this book (plus another book) in your hands now.

I continue to give the Gods offerings of thanks, and I ask for their continued guidance. You can use the below prosperity spell if you need money in a flash. Prosperity spells can be tricky, though. You need to be specific so that you do not have undesired effects. Be open enough in your wording to let money come to you from places and opportunities you may not have thought of yet. Here is a simple spell that fits these requirements.

Let's talk about the wording of this spell so you can see how it works.

The first line is:

Grant me wealth, and grant my wishes,
stir it with a thousand kisses.

This line states the purpose and the way you want your desire to come to you. "With a thousand kisses" means with only love. You make sure that wealth does not come with pain or trouble for anyone.

The second line states:

By the moon, and by the sun,
watch for it, 'cause here it comes

This line uses the powers of the moon and the sun to help accomplish your desire.

The third line says:

It comes by night, it comes by day,
it comes to me with no shades of gray

By mentioning both night and day, the line communicates the intention is that wealth arrives continually.

The phrase "it comes to me with no shades of gray" is very important. The idea of "no shades of gray" means you want wealth to come to you without any negativity associated with it. For example, you want that no one will get into an accident and leave you money.

The fourth line finishes with:

The sea goes in, the sea goes out,
now look at me, my wealth about!

This last line talks about the outcome of the spell. You affirm that you do receive wealth.

The fifth line is simple:

So mote it be!

This line activates the spell.

You can notice that this spell has the power of the five elements in it. I know it isn't obvious. I'll explain. The grant part in the first line comes from Spirit. This refers to your need. This desire arises from your heart. Here is where the process begins.

The second line talks about the heavenly bodies in the sky which is Air. You're placing your thought into the world.

The third line emphasizes no shades of gray or no shadows. Fire is light, and it chases darkness away, banishing the shadows from your wish.

The fourth line is a declaration of manifesting wealth. We

can notice that wealth, in the Tarot, is symbolized as Earth. Further, "the sea goes in, the sea goes out" refers to Water and birthing wealth.

The last line "so mote it be" echoes the second line and plants the entire spell into reality. In effect, it fulfills the desire.

Now that we have discussed the spell and how it works, let's begin. Remember to cast your circle first. If you don't know how to do that read my how to cast circle chapter.

Elemental Money Candle Spell

What you will need:

• Candles in colors: white, yellow, red, blue, and green (representing the elements).
  • Pentacle
  • Matches or lighter
  • Ritual tools

Place candles at appropriate elements on a pentacle.

(Set up your altar and space. Then cast your circle)

Say while lighting the white candle:

> Grant me wealth, and grant my wishes,
> stir it with a thousand kisses.

Light the yellow candle and say:

By the moon, and by the sun,
watch for it, 'cause here it comes.

Light the red candle and say:

It comes by night, it comes by day,
it comes to me with no shades of gray.

Light the blue candle and say:

The sea goes in, the sea goes out,
now look at me, my wealth about!

Light the green candle and say:

So mote it be!

(Do the Cakes and Wine Ceremony)

(Close the circle)

It helps to surround any prosperity spell with positive intentions. What good do you want to do with the prosperity when it comes into your life? A valuable part of a positive intention is "for my good and all those involved."

SECOND CANDLE MONEY SPELL

Here is another example of a simple candle spell you can use for prosperity.

What you will need:

- Your altar
- Your tools
- A script to cast your circle
- Cakes and wine or juice
- A green candle (green is for prosperity, although you may also use gold)
- Matches or a lighter
- Money Oil (oil designed to draw money to you—see below)

To make Money Oil, mix together the following essential oils:

- 1 part ginger
- 2 parts orange
- 1 part pine
- 2 parts cinnamon

- 1/2 part chamomile
- 1 part cedar wood
- 1 part jasmine (optional)

This spell should be done only on the waxing moon. The best time is when the moon is closest to being full.

To do this Money Spell:

1) Cast your circle.

2) Take one green or gold candle.

3) Dress your candle.

"Dress" the candle with the Money Oil. While envisioning money flowing into your life, rub the oil on the candle. Spread the oil from the top of the candle to the center, and then from the bottom back to the center. This technique charges the candle with your will. So be sure to concentrate and take your time with this step.

4) Use the taper to light the green or gold candle from the working candle.

5) Concentrate on the flame. Put your will into it. Take your time.

6) Speak or chant the following:

As I light this candle so,
Make my money grow and grow.
Let it flow without rhyme or reason,

Each and every turn of season.
Filling up my pockets wide,
Let me enjoy this happy ride.
With no malice, woe, or hitches,
May there be no mess with glitches.
Let me have no need for fear of ruin,
Whilst letting go of poverty for fortune,
So mote it be!

A Note About How Positive Intentions Can Free You from Hesitation about Money Spells:

Some people find that trying to manifest more money in their lives seems not spiritual. They may call it selfish. They think that it's about not trying to help others.

But if you're doing a money spell to help create abundance in your life with the intention to help yourself *and others*, it works in a better way!

As I mentioned earlier, I did a spell for more energy to help others and increase my income—and this book is the result.

So become clear about helping others and yourself. If you find yourself hesitating, pull out a sheet of paper and identify *exactly* what you would do with the money. You could even designate 1% to 10% of the money as for some cause, perhaps to help children (if that's your cause).

My point is: Prosperity flows toward certainty. And that's an element of the Law of Attraction. The Law does not respond to tentative efforts. Some instructors talk about the

Law of Attraction as a function of "Ask, Believe, Receive."
You can see how we're called to bring some certainty.

I appreciate a quote that a loved one shared with me.

I could not say I believe [in God]. **I know!** *I have had the experience of being gripped by something that is stronger than myself, something that people call God. - Carl Jung*

The idea about prosperity is: It helps when you write down an actual list of what good things you will do with the money—and what good feelings in yourself and others you will create. Then it's not a matter of a flimsy belief that you will do good with the prosperity. The list helps you **to know.**

How can you see this spell helping you accomplish your goals? It helps to have positive intentions about what you will do with prosperity when it arrives.

CONCLUSION

Through the journey of this book we have looked at the things that block us from success and abundance. We have gained personal insights about these blockages in our lives and have explored tools to help us conquer these barriers.

Looking back on my own journey I have seen myself grow in unexpected leaps and bounds. Starting from a shriveled, unnurtured seed, finding my way to the fertile soil that is Wicca and taking root there. With the nourishment of the Gods' and Goddesses' love I grew strong and became healthy.

I saw myself become the bud, with all the potential of the rose within. Finding the light of self love and respect within I bloomed and became the rose. As the rose I now experience abundance. With Wicca, I became a rose in a beautiful garden of my own making.

Use the tools of grounding, meditation, and the wisdom of the Gods in magick.

If you have questions or comments I would love to hear from you. Askawitchnow@gmail.com

Blessed Be.

- *Moonwater SilverClaw*

ABOUT THE AUTHOR

Moonwater SilverClaw is a Wiccan High Priestess and member of the Covenant of the Goddess and the New Wiccan Church. She has trained people new to Wicca. Her personal story reveals how Wicca saved her life and helped her strengthen herself to secure her release from an abusive marriage.

Moonwater has been practicing Wicca since 1990, first as a solitary and then in a coven.

Moonwater posts at her blog, TheHiddenChildrenoftheGoddess.com

She felt called to write the blog even through she is dyslexic. She works with a team of editors. She says, "I wish to educate those who don't understand what the Craft is about. Some people may not yet identify themselves as pagan, but they'd like more information."

She has addressed college students in Comparative

Religion classes for over ten years. She leads workshops. She lives with her cat Magick and her sweetheart of many years; he is one of her editors. She enjoys knitting and photography.

Her work is endorsed by Wiccan notables including Patrick McCollum (receiver of the Mahatma Gandhi Award for the Advancement of Pluralism).

Moonwater SilverClaw can be contacted at:

AskAWitchNow@gmail.com

Or at her blog:
TheHiddenChildrenoftheGoddess.com

Also from another QuickBreakthrough Publishing Author:

EXCERPT FROM
BE HEARD AND BE TRUSTED:
HOW YOU CAN USE SECRETS OF THE
GREATEST COMMUNICATORS
TO GET WHAT YOU WANT

3rd Edition by Tom Marcoux,
America's Communication Coach

Table of Contents

* * * * * *

Part I, Section 1
How You Can Radiate Charisma
and Get What You Want

What terrific things could be in your life if you were charismatic?

Imagine if you could easily gain people's agreement and cooperation. Top professionals come across as charismatic. *The American Heritage Dictionary* defines "charisma" as "personal magnetism or charm."

A charismatic person makes each of us feel like the most important person in the room. How is this done? The charismatic person listens to others and connects with their pain.

A charismatic person often uses an effective story to engage people's emotions and open listeners to benevolent influence.

A charismatic person expresses compelling messages. Dictionary.com defines "compelling" as "to force or drive, especially to a course of action … to overpower … to have a powerful and irresistible effect, influence." We want to overpower inertia, low moods, and procrastination. We want to take action consistently to create the best possible situations in our own lives.

An interviewer said to me, "I'm not comfortable with the idea of 'force.'"

"All right, let's focus on having a good intention first," I replied. "Instead of force, let's aim to 'move' a person's emotions. "For example, when I was ten years old, my piano teacher knew how to persuade me to practice. She helped me see how much I improved when I practiced. She moved my emotions so that I could feel and enjoy the benefits I was getting. She also cleverly had me practice a song that I really wanted to play."

In essence, my piano teacher was a compelling communicator. She was heard and trusted by me. And that's what you'll learn how to do in this book.

How much would your life improve if you could easily get people to say yes to you? What if you could easily get them to want to say yes?

- "Yes! You're hired. The job is yours."
- "Yes! Here's your raise and promotion."
- "Yes! I'll marry you."
- "Yes! Here's $200,000 to develop your entrepreneurial idea."
- "Yes! I'll buy your product."

What if you could get what you really want – faster than you ever imagined?

That was both the opportunity and the problem for my client Sarah. She confessed, "I need to improve my communication skills."

"How would that give you what you really want?" I asked.

For a moment, she frowned in thought.

"And what do you really want?"

"A raise and a promotion!" she said with sudden clarity.

"What would that take?"

"My boss would have to trust me with higher profile assignments."

In essence, Sarah didn't just want to improve her communication skills; she wanted to be heard and be trusted.

With my guidance, Sarah learned to use the skills found in this book. She learned methods to increase her confidence, speak well to authority, and feel higher self-esteem.

For 26 years, I have helped thousands of clients and audience members become great communicators. In fact, an earlier version of this book was accepted as a textbook by Cogswell Polytechnical College and included in that college's time capsule.

The capsule is set to be opened in 2100. Even in 2100, the timeless principles of warm and trustworthy communication will be valuable.

In this book, we will cover story after story that highlight how many, including twelve billionaires and millionaires, communicate successfully to make things happen. You will also learn directly from the articles and comments of a number of other great communicators.

This book is filled with principles that can help you relate to people on a higher level of connection and cooperation.

As to methods there may be a million and then some, but principles are few. The man who grasps principles can successfully select his own methods. The man who tries methods, ignoring principles, is sure to have trouble. - Ralph Waldo Emerson

For compelling communication, you need to do two things:

1. Seize the attention
2. Create a connection

We want our communication to be not merely pleasant, but compelling. We want people to cooperate with us, to take action in the direction we're proposing. To help you make this year the best year of your life so far, we will explore the C.O.M.P.E.L. process.

C - Connect with the listener's pain
O - Open with genuineness
M - Maximize leverage
P - Pull with a story
E - Ease
L - Lift

"Be so good – they can't ignore you," said writer-actor-comedian Steve Martin in response to the question, "How do you gain big success?" With this book, you will become so good at influencing people. And, I will add, be so trustworthy that they want to do for you.

Let's move on. Let's learn how to be charismatic and influential …

Connect with the Listener's Pain

Where does it hurt? Did your attention go to your body? Did you feel tension in your neck area?

To make your message compelling, you need to uncover your listener's pain.

Ask someone what he or she wants. The easiest way for the person to reply is to say, "What I don't want is to stay in this job.

Here's what I do not like in my current situation." The person talks about what causes pain.

What I have in my heart must come out; that is the reason I compose. - Ludwig van Beethoven

Beethoven reminds us that what is in our hearts must come out. Similarly, as great communicators we need to help our listener express his or her heartfelt pains and desires. By helping your listener identify "where it hurts," you can help her achieve a transformation.

The power of transformation reminds me of the journey of Gay Hendricks, the bestselling author of *Five Wishes* and cofounder of The Hendricks Institute. Years ago, when he was a 300-pound tobacco addict in a horrible marriage, he felt the need to reinvent himself. He says that what sustained him was a deep inner knowledge of where he was going – toward a life of soul awareness and creative fulfillment. Today he has a fit,

180-pound frame, over six feet tall. Gay was blocked. His blockage was made of conflicted feelings: he couldn't decide whether to continue studying in the University of New Hampshire counseling program or follow his desire to be a writer. Dwight Webb, an insightful professor of his, suggested, "Why not write about counseling?" Was there any reason Gay could not put his feelings and inner experiences into poems and articles connected with his profession? The answer was that he could do both things he loved. He could pursue psychological counseling and writing. Gay's poems were published in counseling journals and caught the eye of a professor at Stanford University, who helped Gay gain a fellowship to that institution for his doctorate. Gay went on to a 25-year academic career and wrote over 20 books.

When I contacted Gay a while ago, I discovered that he had found fulfillment as a screenwriter-filmmaker and as a seminar leader through The Hendricks Institute. Gay's journey shows that it is an "and" universe, not a "this or that" universe. The point is that Gay's professor Dwight Webb provided great coaching. He listened to Gay's pain and shared a new way to view the situation.

The only service a friend can really render is to keep up your courage by holding up to you a mirror in which you can see a noble image of yourself. - George Bernard Shaw

When you really want to be heard and be trusted, focus on something that will benefit the other person. Be the person's friend. Take the appropriate actions to help him or her.

With a number of my clients, we focus on the transition from novice salesperson to coach-to-action. As George Bernard Shaw points out, you as the coach can hold a friendly mirror up to your listener, who will then be able to see a noble image of the self. This noble image can inspire the listener to agree to whatever you're offering. And as the coach, you can help the person enjoy more in life and work.

It is above all by the imagination that we achieve perception and compassion and hope. - Ursula LeGuin

First, connect with the listener's pain. Then, with the knowledge you have gained, you can focus on helping. You can help people imagine a better personal future.

People in general are starved for the experience of being heard. - Gordon Livingston, M.D.

Get what you want by giving people what they crave: to be heard.

Principle:
Connect with the listener's pain and show that you have the remedy.

Power Question:
How can you gently ask questions that allow you to identify the listener's pain?*

*NOTE: * To get the maximum benefit from this book, devote at least 20 seconds to writing down the answer to each Power Question in your personal journal.*

Open with Genuineness

When you are content to be simply yourself and don't compare or compete, everybody will respect you. - Lao-tzu

"We don't need you to be perfect; we need you to be genuine," I say to my graduate students who seek to be better public speakers and pitch-givers.

Do what you said you were going to do,
when you said you were going to do it,
in exactly the way you said you were going to do it.
You won't ever get any better business advice than that.
Be there when you said you would be there.
Deliver when you said you would deliver.
Call when you said you would call.
Be a person who can be counted on
by keeping his word every time.
- Larry Winget

Have you ever been afraid that when you are giving a speech, your mind might go blank or you might lose your place? The solution is, *be genuine.*

When I coach CEOs and company presidents in how to give speeches, I help them express genuineness. This helps the CEO connect with the audience and motivate team members.

End of Excerpt from
Be Heard and Be Trusted: How You Can Use Secrets of the Greatest Communicators to Get What You Want
Copyright 2012 Tom Marcoux Media, LLC

Purchase your copy of this book (paperback or ebook) at Amazon.com or BarnesandNoble.com
See **Free Chapters** of Tom Marcoux's 21 books
at http://amzn.to/ZiCTRj

Special Offer Just for Readers of this Book:
Contact Moonwater SilverClaw at
askawitchnow@gmail.com for special discounts on books, consultations, workshops and presentations. Just mention your experience with this book. Thank you.

www.ingramcontent.com/pod-product-compliance
Lightning Source LLC
LaVergne TN
LVHW021513080426
835509LV00018B/2499